GETTING READY FOR NEW BABY

By Harriet Ziefert Pictures by Laura Rader

Harper & Row, Publishers

Text copyright © 1990 by Harriet Ziefert
Illustrations copyright © 1990 by Laura Rader
Printed in Singapore for Harriet Ziefert, Inc.
All rights reserved.
1   2   3   4   5   6   7   8   9   10
First Edition
CIP data available.
ISBN 0-06-026896-4.—ISBN 0-06-026897-2 (lib. bdg.)
Library of Congress Catalog Card Number: 90-32197

CONTENTS

Why a New Baby?

One day your parents may come to you and say:
Mommy is going to have a baby in a few months.

You may wonder why your parents want another baby.
Why do they need one?

It's not easy to understand why your parents want another child. Have you ever heard your mother say, "I like being a mommy—your Mommy." And have you ever heard your father say, "I like being a daddy—your Daddy." Because your parents like being parents—your parents—they want another child.

Do you wonder how the baby got inside your mother? Do you also wonder if the baby is a boy or a girl?

Do you wonder where the new baby will sleep? Will it be in your old crib?

Do you wonder when the baby will be born?

In winter?

In spring?

In summer?

In fall?

Good Feelings, Not-so-Good Feelings

When a new baby is coming, look at all the feelings:

excited

mixed-up

afraid

angry

curious

jealous

worried

happy

Feelings keep changing. Sometimes you have good feelings; sometimes not-so-good ones. But there are things you can do about the not-so-good feelings.

It's okay to say how angry you are.

It helps to talk about your feelings.

When you are mixed up, it's good to ask questions. You may want to ask your mother: How did the baby get in there? Who's going to get it out? Will it get stuck?

You could ask your father: How do you make a baby?
Can I make a baby?

Your parents will try to answer your questions.

And they will help you find answers in books.

How Babies Are Made

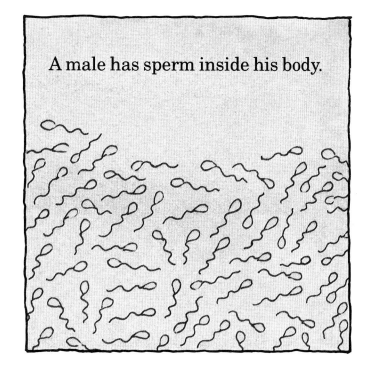

A male has sperm inside his body.

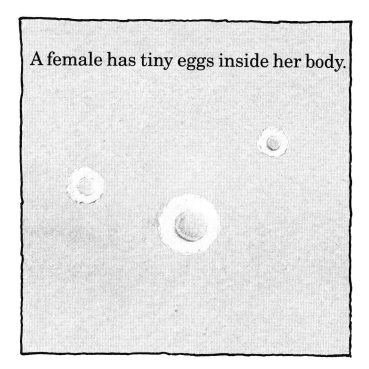

A female has tiny eggs inside her body.

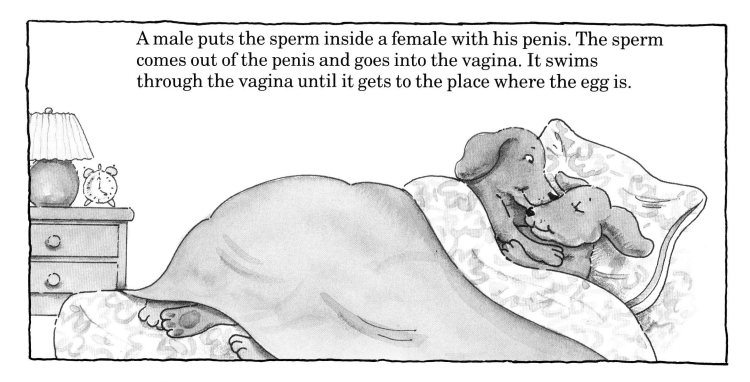

A male puts the sperm inside a female with his penis. The sperm comes out of the penis and goes into the vagina. It swims through the vagina until it gets to the place where the egg is.

A sperm and an egg join together inside a mother and a baby begins.

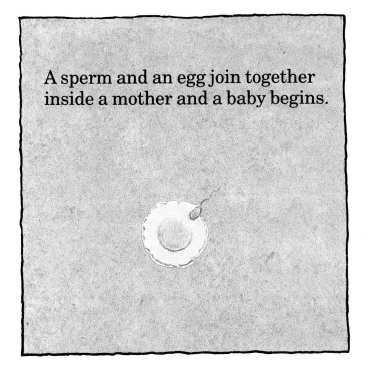

The baby that begins inside a mother grows in a special place. The place is called the womb.

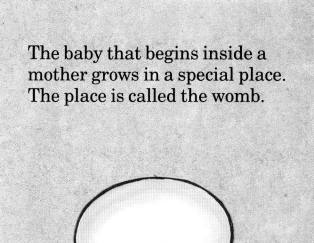

The baby grows in a mother's womb. It grows bigger and bigger.

The baby grows until there is no more room. Then it is time for the baby to be born.

It takes a male cricket and a female cricket to make a baby cricket.

It takes a male bird and a female bird to make a baby bird.

It takes a male snake and a female snake to make a baby snake.

It takes a male monkey and a female monkey to make a baby monkey.

Children can't make babies. Boys' bodies don't make sperm; and inside girls' bodies, the eggs aren't ready yet. Children have to grow up. Then they can become mothers and fathers.

The Baby Is Born

When your mother goes to the hospital to have the baby, you may feel left out because you can't go along.

But as soon as the baby is born, you can visit your mother and the new baby.

You can see what the baby looks like.

You can ask the nurse to pick up the baby
so you can see it better.

The Baby Comes Home

After a few days, your parents will bring the baby home.

Sometimes the baby will cry.

The baby will sleep a lot.

Some babies drink milk from bottles. Others nurse. When your mother nurses the baby, you may feel left out. You may want to taste your mother's milk. Maybe she will put some in a cup for you.

Dos and Don'ts

Some things to do and some things not to do:

Talk and sing to the baby.

But don't make loud noises near the baby.

Hold the baby's hand.

Tickle the baby's toes.

Give the baby a pacifier. Make the baby feel cozy.
But don't climb into the baby's crib.

Smile and make funny faces.

Wind up the baby's mobile.

Push the baby's stroller.

But don't push it too hard.

You can help give the baby a bath.

You can show the baby a toy.

A new baby does not go back to the hospital.
It stays forever. But your parents still love you.
That doesn't change when a new baby arrives.

Some Things Change

Your parents will ask you to do more things for yourself.
You're big. You can dress yourself.

And feed yourself.

And wash yourself.

But you don't have to do everything by yourself.

Your parents will still help you.

You don't have to act like a baby to get attention.

Your parents will read with you…

and play games…

and take you shopping…

and out to eat.

The Baby Grows

Your baby will learn to:

smile

babble and coo

roll over

sit up

grab

pull

crawl

stand

Getting Along with a Growing Baby

Now you have to watch out for your stuff!

Babies knock things over.

They chew things.

They tear things.

But you're older and bigger.

You can hide things you care about.

You can work at a table or desk.

You can close the door. It's good to be alone sometimes.

But when you don't want to be alone, there's someone around:

Someone to stay home with when the babysitter comes...

someone to be the patient
so you can be the doctor...

someone to be the robber
so you can be the cop.

someone to have fights with...

someone to love.

With a new baby in the family, everyone's love grows.